A Burst of Sunshine

by

Anthony Mondal

RoseDog ❧ Books
PITTSBURGH, PENNSYLVANIA 15222

The contents of this work including, but not limited to, the accuracy of events, people, and places depicted; opinions expressed; permission to use previously published materials included; and any advice given or actions advocated are solely the responsibility of the author, who assumes all liability for said work and indemnifies the publisher against any claims stemming from publication of the work.

All Rights Reserved
Copyright © 2012 by Anthony Mondal

No part of this book may be reproduced or transmitted, downloaded, distributed, reverse engineered, or stored in or introduced into any information storage and retrieval system, in any form or by any means, including photocopying and recording, whether electronic or mechanical, now known or hereinafter invented without permission in writing from the publisher.

RoseDog Books
701 Smithfield Street
Pittsburgh, PA 15222
Visit our website at *www.rosedogbookstore.com*

ISBN: 978-1-4349-7338-2
eISBN: 978-1-4349-2049-2

Preface: A Burst of Sunshine

A Burst of Sunshine is my second book of a collection of poems and I wish to dedicate this book to both my parents (father and mother respectively). Well they are both now dead and long gone…but somehow life goes on and their beautiful memories are still scattered all over, like flower petals as blessings showering over my head.

As I sit down to write an introduction for this book, a burst of sunshine hits my writing desk. The warm rays of sunshine falls on my face and arms… my heart and soul…Awakening my whole being from slumber and tiredness.

Is it too much or too ambitious to hope that such a positive and beneficial effect may also befall the readers of this book? The book is also dedicated to Sensitive Kind and Intelligent people, women men boys and girls from all walks of life…for in them lies the dreams hopes and futures of a better Tomorrow.
Let Light prevail and Darkness be gone.

Anthony Mondal (Author)
27/02/2011

Table of Contents

1. The Dilemma of life 1
2. Unconscious Images / Images chosen at Random from a Millennium Night 2
3. Ode to a River 3
4. Change 4
5. Song of a Caged bird. 5
6. Broken – Heart 6
7. Knock, Knock.....Knocking 7
8. To Solitude 8
9. The Blessed Rain. 9
10. Futility 10
11. The Coming of Spring 11
12. The Sound of my Soul 12
13. Devaluation? 13
14. Angel Faced Orphans 14
15. A tribute to Woman and Gold 15
16. Vicious charm 16
17. And This Moment Fades, Away. 17
18. Soldiers of Life 18
19. A Topsy Turvy world 19
20. The Unsung Heroes 20
21. Time 21
22. The City Nights 22
23. The Businessman's Mantra As Distilled From The Television 23
24. Ode to a Sunset 24

25.	The path way of Dream	25
26.	Beauty shines Her light	26
27.	To Freedom	27
28.	An Autumn Moment	28
29.	Yester – days	29
30.	To performers of the City Streets	30
31.	In Spite Of	31
32.	Minority	32
33.	A visit to Mrs. Susan	33
34.	Circles	35
35.	Between Sanity & Insanity	36
36.	Scenes from a construction site	37
37.	The Business of late fall	38
38.	I Don't wish to live like a Refugee	39
39.	The Spectrum	40
40.	Sunday Morning Music show	41
41.	Waiting for Answers	42
42.	The Runaway Girl	43
43.	Sacred or Profane?	44
44.	That Guilty feeling....	45
45.	A love affair in Central Park	46
46.	The Holiday Blues	47
47.	Bits and pieces of conversation in an Uptown Train	48
48.	In Search of the Artist	49
49.	Who will Fix it? Who will Mend?	50
50.	A Modern Poem	51
51.	A torn page from my childhood	52
52.	Far away from the civilization	53
53.	The Tale of John Kalahas	54
54.	9 –11 Poem	56
55.	A Poem dedicated to Peace	57

The Dilemma of Life

Is life just an illusion?
Where human beings are in total delusion
Or is it the vision of an ever better tomorrow
Which never seems to come.

Is life just mere formality?
A place where people worship artificial decency
Or is it about utmost sincerity
Which holds up our integrity and human dignity.

Is life just shattered dreams?
Where more dreams are discouraged than encouraged
Or is it the perseverance towards one's dreams
Which give significance to an individual's worth.

Is life just fragmented events at random?
A place of chaos and mayhem,
Or is it fragments fused invisibly by the hand of God,
To make sense of the order that lies amidst the chaos.

Is life just mere apathetic utter Ignorance?
Where many dwell in stupendous Arrogance
Or is it the brilliance of Knowledge
That illuminates our life like a new Sunrise.

Unconscious Images / Images Chosen At Random From A Millennium Night

Cold cold Night
Howling Winds
The wailing cats
The bitter chills
The restless Poet
Sleepless Artist,
Wide Awake and Alive
With their failures and their frights.
The Homeless Weeps
A mother wakes up for the morning chores
The Birth of Dawn
And the dark night flees
Faint rays of light
Greet the city streets
Purified Hope on the Horizon
Rinse away all the city poisons
Another Morning
Another Beginning.

Ode to a River

As I sit in solitude by her side
The morning rays of sunshine sets the river alive
The heavenly clouds from above they peer
Softly into hear ears the wind whisper

And she replies gently with a murmur
Life a youthful maiden, shy yet brave
With eyes open wide in curious delight
She continues her voyage with courage and might

Like an adorned princess so complete in grace
In path unforeseen, she offers herself again and again.
In her sweet genteel playful moods
She blesses everything by her touch
And in occasional angrier times
She outbursts her emotions, in ravage and destruction much
But only to forgive and be forgotten soon enough.

As I watch her flow by in spellbound captivity
Lo, behold, I never come across such a beauty
Slowly as the vision fades away,
Imperfect thoughts hovering in mind
I try to trace her origins
But from whence she comes nobody knows.

Change

As the seasons come and go
Bringing us abundance as well as scarcity
So also in Man's life
There are season's of joy and melancholy
From birth till death
Change leads us all the way
Necessary is change, and at times a necessity
Change we must, in tune with the clock of Nature
Or else be left, as are Ghosts of the ancient relics
For only a miser of life, stubbornly holds on to life's furniture
Change is that which keeps Hope alive
For a great future that awaits mankind
Change my friend is the very game of life
Without change life can't survive.

The Song of a Caged Bird

A bright yellow canary bird
With traces of blue and beak pink;
Captive she was, her conditions bleak,
Running around in her cage iron black
Searching for escape, that's a fact,
A great song bird she was, in her days wild
No sooner thrust in cage, her songs declined,
Now barely able to flap her wings
How unfair of us, expecting her to sing!
Numerous times, she appealed for freedom
But to no avail, was given attention seldom,
Like a circus clown, we wanted her to perform
Entertain us, when she would rather in sorrows drown,
Then one bright morning, as we gathered round the cage
To our great dismay found
Her prayers have been granted
The song bird forever has left the cage.

Broken – Heart

*I can't carry any longer
These pieces of my broken heart much further.
There was a time, when all was one
Now I am divided, and incomplete as anyone.*

Knock Knock ...... Knocking

Many a doors have I knocked
Some answered me, and some did not
And some doors, on my face have been shut,
Yet I keep on searching and seeking
For that Door, welcoming me with arms wide open.

To Solitude

From the very early years in my life
You walked into my heart and made your home
Now that I have traveled with you so far
Having lost and gained, plenty friends here and there
But none to me is ever so near.
True it is, though hard to believe
Even when I curse thee, for being deceived
Thine silent whispers, with gratitude I receive.

O, for without their soft guidance
I would have long ere perished to Be.

The Blessed Rain

The stormy winds gives dust wings
Precariously low the gray clouds hang
At a distance I hear the thundering bangs
A flash of lightning across the sky streaks

Rain drops falls on trembling tree leaves
On the river, the meadow, and the valley steep
Forests beasts and birds, together they dance
Setting aside, their differences for a while

In rain drops, the thirsty earth bathes
What heavenly music my ears arrest
O what a splendid concert Mother Nature conducts
Where every rhythm, harmony and beat is intact.

As an arid desert plant for water desire (Th).
So does my heart awaits, for rain drops from above
Cleanse and wash away my tribulations and sin
Make me feel alive again, come and make me sing.

Futility

Streams of clouds, like boats
Floats across the ocean of blue sky
The autumn golden yellow leaves
They shine in triumphant glory.
Verily on the verge of its Death
Soon only, to wither and fall away.
Suddenly a wave of sadness overwhelmed my soul.
Grief inexplicable, beyond words to be told.
And with tireless eyes I probe, for a friendly face
In crowds of people, of our lonely human race
The last drop of day light
Was squeezed out from my sight.
Another nights falls – with a heavy heart
I lay my head down to rest.

The Coming of Spring

I woke up to the chorus of birds singing
Joyfully they announce, the advent of spring
I open my eyes and behold the glorious sunshine.
Hills, vales and flowers are smiling;
A lake nearby reflects the azure sky.
As if a magician with his magic wand
In the depths of night touched
And Earth desolate, to a garden of paradise transformed.
Gently blown by the perfumed spring breeze,
Oh so glad my being feels!
Joy herself rushing thru my bloods and veins.
Surrounded by pleasant sceneries and sounds;
On the wings of dream myself I found;
Transported to a colorful fairy play ground.

The Sound of My Soul

O, my weary wayward Soul,
Longs to be homeward bound,
But Home? No where can be found.
Searching for shelter
Searching for peace
But this ruthless world pays me no heed.

O, my weary wayward Soul,
Longs for rest in this restless world,
Like a lonely seagull, lost in the cloud,
Searching for the path
Searching for friends.
But all my search in vain it ends

O, my weary wayward Soul,
Longs for kindness, longs for compassion.
But a voice inside says it is a waste of passion
Searching for strength
Searching for courage
As I trudge along thru' this endless tunnel of grief discouraged.

O, my weary wayward Soul,
Longs for freedom, longs for salvation
But bondage and persecution are my only option
Searching for humanity
Searching for divinity
All I receive from both is nothing but pity.

Devaluation?

In the market places of this world;
Where life as a cheap commodity sold.
Buyers and Sellers, aye there are plenty
But few are those, who appreciates life's worth fully.

Angel Faced Orphans

While browsing thru a magazine once,
I turned a page, and their they were;
A young girl not more than five,
With an even younger brother, by her side.
Weeping bitterly among strangers unknown;
For their departed parents, they mourn.
Love snatched away, and their innocence betrayed
Scarred emotionally at such a tender age;
What chances do they have?
To survive this battle field of life ahead.
Their parents murdered in cold blood.
And their dwellings burnt!
Over what? But two bits of land.
Rich they were not before;
But at least, they were not poor
Now Orphaned and wretchedly poor,
To live, they must beg door to door
Unless kindness and empathy comes their way
These homeless orphans have nowhere to stay.
Hard it is, to grow up, in this ever changing world.
With all the comforts and the care
Imagine, how hard it might yet be
For those Orphaned kids,
With no one for them to care.
God, Thou art supremely benevolent
Then, why have you forsaken them?
What good may arise, from such brutal pain?

A Tribute to Women and Gold

Beautiful women and Glittering Gold
Makes the world go round and round;
From a time long, long ago.
A pretty Woman and a little Gold;
We all know?
Will lead many a men to sell their soul.
Though verily, this lust for Women and Gold
Is the driving force, behind this chariot of Mankind.
Truly without which, there would be
No un – folding of the history of Mankind.
It is the sole impetus of the explorers;
The urge of Great Conquerors;
The only passion known to painters, Artists
And Poets in multitude.
Without Gold and Without Women
Earth would still be a dwelling
But a prison house, with walls strange and unknown:
So with a heart gratified:
I pay my indebted respect and tribute.
To all the Women and Gold;
Past, present and future I salute.
Without them, mankind would have nothing to contribute.

Vicious Charm

Her face, a feast for the eyes
Her smile seems like a warm sunshine
Hopelessly and helplessly you fall for her charm
Too late you realize
You are a trapped insect in a giant spider web
And she penetrates her poisonous venoms
On the victim's soft breast.
Effortlessly she glides over, always supremely efficient
As she moves on from one victim to the next.

And This Moment Fades Away.......

*Brighter Tomorrows
And Golden Yester – days.
But all we have right Now
Is nothing ——
But this moment Today.*

Soldiers of Life

Dream on Dream on, O Soldier of life
This world is but a space, that in your mind occupies.
Carry on Carry on with your revolt and optimism.
Do not be discouraged
And a New World will wash away, all the old World – isms.
Tyrants they come and tyrants they go
Truth still shines, though the progress is slow.
You carry the weight, You carry the burden
You blast the path and dark roads brighten.
None but you may fulfill this task
So don't abandon your Dreams, that is all I ask.

A Topsy Turvy World

Fish they nest up in the trees
Birds swim deep in the blue sea's.
Men and women live in forests naked
While the beasts walk around in suits well dressed.
People walk with their legs held high in the air
And the heads they are dragged on ground
The sky is below and the ocean above
Somehow it just does not rain and drench us all.
The moon blazes during the day
And the sun throughout the night dazzles.
And the change of seasons, they are seen no more
Curiously I watch the scenes unfold, trying to make some sense
Then it dawned unto me
Oh it is a topsy turvy world!
Born out of a mere fragment of my Imagination
And nothing more at all.

The Unsung Heroes

Our world is filled with Unsung Heroes
Though they never make it to the newspaper page
So I picked up my pen, for their cause;
And sing a song, for their Goodness sake
Universal are these few good women and men
Never confined to any one race, nation or religion.
The Painter, carpenter and the mechanic
Not to forget mothers, fathers, and wives
You will meet them, in every path of life;
Like stars on a clear night they shine;
Conscientious in work and shy by nature
Firm determination, courageous under pressure
Unmindful to who so ever they serve
Their hands are steady and strong are their nerves.
Only thru them is well preserved, the lamp of Hope.
For a greater and brighter hope to come
Their sweet smile will soothe, all your wear and tears
If you only extend your hand without any fear.
Behind their kindness unpolluted
You will see the smiling face and hands of God
They are like islands of sanity, in a world gone mad.

Time

Time from the ancient past and the present
Keeps fleeting in motion
For the future that is yet to be
Ever making and ever breaking
Towards the path of the future unforeseen.

Many a human heart crushed and broken under, it.
Whose stories never told and lost
In the abyss of the tunnel called Time,
Though it appears to be cruel and monstrous,
But it must move on towards its endless Destiny.

The City Nights

In the middle of the night, outside I stepped
Shops are closed and streets deserted.
The neon lights shine, dazzlingly bright;
And will shine on, remainder of the night;
Unconcerned about anyone,
For silent spectators are they, of tragedies committed out of our sight

Many a young heart, the city traps
Enchanted by her gloss and glamour;
Failing to see her cold and deceptive manners.
Speeding cars rush thru the night,
Leaving behind streams of light.
Yonder I hear music playing.

Also sirens of ambulance and police cars wailing
For a moment I thought, an old woman weeping.
Thru the scenes of frolic of the city night
I see the face of a woman in plight.
She appears to be pretty, at first glance
But on closer inspection, her cosmetic mask fades away
Revealing her age, and wrinkles of skin ugly.
Stands before me an elderly prostitute;
For long she had her body abused.

Wandering aimlessly on the city streets, in agony of shame and defeat;
The hollow laughter's of frolicking women, in my head, they repeat.
Towers of steel and glass surround us in plenty,
Nay, they dwarf and ridicule our very own individuality.
And the cool night wind, from every direction brings,
To my ear, the sighs and groans of disconnected lives,
Chained in their self imposed glass cages.
And the city continues to be at war, in rages.

A Businessman's Mantra As Distilled From The Television

Coupons Rebate Discount Sale
Sale Sale Sell Sell
Everything is going so well!
50% off 40% off, $1000 down payment
Look at my hair! Look at my dress
Look at my Skin! Look at Me!
Look at me, look at me as well.
(Give me your money, now get up and Shop!)
(Buy name brands only Please)
I hope you got the above subliminal message.
You are in my grip, Now you are in my control
I possess your body, Nay I possess your soul
You have no mind you have no backbone
Buy car clothes jewelries for evermore ....
My Greed is insatiable And my desires knows no bound.
No need to panic, Oh my very happy perky consumers;
Everything is well Everything is fine
To the miseries of this world pay them no mind.
Please don't wake up – sleep walk thru life
And I promise you, I will cure all the world's ill
If you please continue —- to shopping still.

Ode to a Sunset

As the sun sets slowly over the western sky
It appears as if thousand golden chariots of fire
Leaving behind their blazing trail
As I look beyond, where the ocean meets the sky,
The horizon appears illuminated as if with divine brilliance.
Though the kindled sky at dusk haunts many a poetic soul
The eternal mystery and the majestic beauty of the sunset:
Still remains elusive to the comprehension of mortal beings.
From time knows when? As surely as the sun goes down
(With hopes, aspirations and dreams) in the western sky,
It will rise again in the eastern sky at the break of dawn!
With renewed Hopes, Aspirations and Promises to Humanity.

The Pathway of Dream

The pathway to my dream abode.
Is scattered with broken glasses and discord,
My feet bleeds and my body aches;
Still I must go on, no matter what it takes,
With heart down trodden and soul agonized.
O lord! How much farther till I subside?

Beauty shines Her light

A soft white butterfly
Flutters her wings
And gently rests on the steel rail tracks
A white flower blossoms on the subway walls
Who sustains these strange entities?
Wherein lies their purpose and strength?
A quick glance at them and I regain all my strength....

.......Beauty shines her light in strange nooks and corners
For wayward poets and prophets to behold and discover.

To Freedom

Freedom, freedom, our soul laments
Though we pay him no heed
Dependence, our flesh demands
And is given attention indeed.

Freedom is longed for and freedom coveted
Though we hardly know her ways and needs
And in times of momentous decisions
Ready we are to adopt, the convenience of skin.

Freedom is what we strive for
Freedom, only goal of ours
Alas all is lot in haze
As we lose our ways in tangled webs of mazes,

Quick we are to plunge in battle
In thy name of revolution and freedom supreme.
But we neglect the battle fields of mind
Where the true war goes on, and thy victor to great height ascends.

An Autumn Moment

The gentle autumn breeze is blowing under the big blue sky.
The withered and wrinkled leaves fall away from the trees,
An old woman with her shriveled puppy
Finds no peace in the autumn breeze!

Seasons keep changing and the time passes by;
Many a change of season has come and gone thru her life,
But at this very moment
Both nature and season seems to be frozen in time,
As I look deep in her blue autumn eyes.

Yester —— days

Those dream like days of my early boyhood
How may I ever forget them
For – ever, are they etched in my memory
By a great Artist Unknown.

Those dream like days of my early boyhood
Happy days of endless games and play
And at evenings end,
When sweet slumber banished me to the land of sleep
Overzealous I was, for the morning rays to peep.

Those dream like days of my early boyhood
Oh, how much fun I had had
But sooner or later, the fun and merriment ends
As responsibilities of adult life, on his shoulder descends.

Those dream like days of my early boyhood
How I wish, they were never gone
But only forward, life knows how to march ahead
And knows not the ways, for who falls behind.

To Performers of the City Streets

Performers of the city streets
Display they, a lot of guts;
Yet no glory ever does, pay him a visit
Skillfully does he perform, on Instruments
Like guitar, drums and violin
And many other instruments
Which is all quite hard to explain!
Sometimes he sings, with a cup full of coins
And sometimes he just claps with the motion of the train
He sings duet, and even – quartets – quite often
Charming the audience, with their sense of rhythm.
And they try to sing their bitter sweet songs
While the deafening noise of wheels, on the metal tracks
Crushes all their hopes – and dreams...
Folk singer and Musicians of city streets
Let's not forget dancers, acrobats...
And magicians with tricks.
Kind are many city people
In appreciating what they do
But then there are others
Unkind, impolite and mean spirited too.
From one struggling artist to another
I do so understand.
Where they are coming from
Lured are they to city streets,
For lack of money and right opportunities
And needs not to be perceived, as beggar and a nuisance
For they do deserve our compassion and tolerance.

In Spite Of

Though no one takes notice
No one is aware
Yet spring still comes, with her leafy green robe.

The rivers, with wanton carelessness we pollute
But still they run to greet the sea.

The forest trees, ruthlessly are they brought down
Yet they shower us with fruits, and birds to sing

And the blue sky, not spared from man's progressive hands
Where toxic fumes are profusely dumped.
Forgets not to bring rain clouds and crystal clear drops of rain.

Though I throw tantrums, like a spoilt kid
You still kindly to me smile
Like a benevolent father to his child.

Minority

I don't know when the Division started
They day when man's soul was bargained
Echoes of voices from long past, asking for pity
Probably when villages were replaced by cities;
Because they wanted to adorn you with urban profanities.
And continuing thru the present times
They keep on labeling and trivializing;
Unconsciously magnifying their own insecurity;
Ever constructing great walls of enmity.
Fear not ye down trodden humanity
For you belong in good company.
The true architects and builders of the heavenly city
Prophets, Poets, and Artists of yester years
Were also once, outcast of the society
Serving boldly Truth, Justice and eternal Beauty.
So proud most definitely, I am, to be considered minority
In this world of spell bound grave digging majority.

A Visit to Mrs. Susan

*I once knew an elderly lady
Seventy two years of age was she,
But she was very, very dear to me.
It seems only few days ago
I paid a visit, at her old age home
Glad she was, to see me come
Affectionately called me, "my young knight handsome,"
A beautiful sunny spring day it was
Perfect for a little walk.
Various things did we talk about
Her memories of glorious youth
Warm stories of her days in south.
Frail in body she may have been
But bright in spirits she was for certain.
Exclaiming in delight
At the sight of spring flowers bloom,
Then I saw her sigh
Probably remembering her days gone by.
Talked she for hours long
Like a chirping bird with a pleasant song.*

*Her own son's and daughter's resided out of state
Abandoned and solitary was she with her sad fate,
Many a times, I have seen her empty stares
Gazing endlessly on the path, outside her window
Hoping her children would come and share
The trials and tribulations of her daily life.
Unfortunately, they never came.
Too busy they were, with their own lives
No time they had, to be bothered about such trifles.
Little do they know, that Age
Knows no friend nor foe
And one day will catch up with them also!
So she died unknown to the world
Passing away peacefully in her sleep.
Bu in my heart she has a very special place*

Lonely but compassionate woman, with a kind face.
Her smile was warm
And so was her heart
Alive in my memories is Lady Susan,
Who often reminded me of an exiled queen, from a far away land.
"Shalom" I said to her in spirit
Bidding my last fare well to Mrs. Susan Ruben stein brave
As I placed the flowers on top of her grave.

Circles

Everywhere I look, Circles, circles all around me
Ever narrow and confining
Their unseen chords suffocating many;
Trapped lives filled with silent misery.
As human seeds into this circular earth we are planted,
In mother's womb nourished;
Which is but a round space enclosed
And therefore from birth, our search begins
For circles of various shapes and sizes,
Till death steals our life away,
We enter schools and colleges
Join prestigious institutions
But never do we feel like, tearing out this envelop of darkness
For great fear of the unknown, still clouds our mind.
Forget people in their love for institutions
Was once, one man's dream in isolation
And in only standing apart alone
He may find his purpose as an individual
An interesting irony of human life cycle.

Between Sanity & Insanity

In this world of vanity, where Appearance
Is preferred over basic human dignity,
Combined with our ways of Inhuman cruelty;
Creates a confused world of distorted Reality,
Where each passing moment,
Thrusts me nearer to Insanity.
Please Lord, I ask with all humility
Pray, tell me how may I keep my sanity?

Scenes from a Construction Site

Early in morning, people come to work
Heavy machineries gnawing into the earth.
Nails driven by carpenters, on wooden planks
The welding – man, iron beams welds
Scattered all over are things many
Bricks, stones and mounds of earth plenty.
Busy is the place, with buzz of work
Like a beehive where bees are at work.
Seven to five they toil everyday
Six days a week, except for Sunday.

Unending are these laboring hands
Generations after generations they come;
Chipping away at the rocks and stones.
The very same hand
Who with their sweat and blood
Once built Pyramids and Tajmahal
Construct they now, great architectures of steel.
Proving once again, work the very nature of soul
Without work it has no goal.
And they build and rebuild
Changing and shaping the world around.

I sit by the window, wrapped in thoughts
As time slowly onward creeps
The noise cease.
Another day has come to an end.
Home ward bound, the workers
Throw me a weary smile
Ashamed I feel of my hours idle;
Yet somehow I also feel
Wasted not, are my solitary thoughts
But time priceless gained.

The Business of Late Fall

The late Autumn stormy winds
Lays the garden waste
The fallen flowers and leaves,
They return to dust
The squirrel for winter, gathers ripened nuts
And the farmers his golden crops in granary stores
The birds fly away in search of warm southern groves
O make haste make haste
No time do we have to waste
Hope and optimism, still awaits outside your door
Hurry or soon winter with vengeance, will be back once more.

I Don't wish to live like a Refugee

I am sitting in an American garden (though done in Japanese style)
The blue sky peeks thru the leafy trees.
Chipmunks they are lazing on the tree trunk, warmed by the sun.
Next to me is a natural fish pond-surrounded by stones-where gold fishes play.
And yet all these natural beauty does not put my mind at rest.
As I pine for quick fix solutions and security.
Tired of wandering and living vagabond existence from suitcases.
At this point in my life-A Refugee holds much more respectability,
And more possessions than me.

The Spectrum

Violet is the color, that burns in my mind
When passion myself finds
Forget I everything, in a blink of an eye.

Indigo is its next stage
While passion in me fades
As I look at the world, thru its kaleidoscopic shades

Blue – oh my eternal blue skies
Calm and peace and endless daydreams
And the world resounds with laughter, up to the brims

Green, evergreen the earth seems to be
All the leaves, each blades of grass and flowers are new
With youthful joy and exuberance my mind flew

Yellow, Oh so pale, sickly yellow- ed
Again and again all my hopes and dreams are crushed
With nothing left for me to trust

Orange glow colors my mind
While I myself to tears and fate resign
Sacrificing myself to hands divine

Red blood Red turns the colors
Rage and Destruction forever
My mind dwells on, and suffer.

Sunday Morning Music Show

The old Saxophone player, on a Sunday Morning
Found his perfect audience at last.
Weary from years and years of hard struggle
Unaware of his surroundings, he serenades
The indifferent Sunday morning crowd.
At times he plays a little too high
Over anxious to please, he missed a note or two
But None can his earnest passion deny.
And he played a sad but haunting tune.
Finishing his piece of music,
Before the train arrives at the platform soon.

Waiting for Answers

Who has clipped my wings of freedom?
Who has stolen all my laughter and joys?
Who is letting me drown in my sorrows and tears?
O Heaven do you have the Answers?
Which so desperately I need
And the sky remains mute and dumb
And the river flows endlessly
The trees they nod their heads in breeze
While I wait ...... and wait ..... and wait
For the Answers to come back to me.

The Runaway Girl

Sixteen years of age, she may be scarcely
Ran away she from home to find her Destiny.
May be a war of words, a pointless argument
Unpleasant things said, in heat of the moment
Was reason enough for her, to run away from the parents.
Now she stands by the door, of the moving car
Her pride wounded and her lower lips quiver
Like a bleeding fawn she shivers.
No place to run, Nowhere to hide
Fleeing from the hunter's arrow, the lion's den she finds.
As if she wakes up from a dream sweet
And discovers herself in a planet
Where to each other we are strangers, who must never meet.
Where, where does lie the solution?
Chances are she will end up, in prostitution.
And in the papers the following day
Ran an ad, under her picture it says
"My dear sweet Caroline
O won't you please to home return.
My Child, My daughter, My angel divine."

Sacred or Profane?

Aye what is vulgar?
And what is profane?
For even the most vulgar and profain
Have origin, in Sacred's domain.
Not without a purpose, No things in vain
Understanding this, peace will your mind attain.

That Guilty Feeling....

That guilty feeling is back again;
Though I understand not, for what exact reason
Could it be, because this gluttony;
Engulfing us, causing abiding misery.
Where the voice of Conscience, but in apathy drowns.
And words of human kindness, like deceit and mockery sounds.
If ever too long, a man (or nation) treads on this path forbidden
His self with certainty, will soon meet its end.

A Love Affair In Central Park

The soft whisperings of sweet nothings & lullaby's into her ear
The gentle brushing of her unruly mane
And he cleans her hooves with his very own hands
While she protests mildly like a child
Then he held her head in his hands
And showered kisses on her lips
She responds by nodding her head in approval.
And the old man passes for nothing
Dressed in shabby clothes with an awkward gait
But if only our eyes could see,
The love of the old man for his horse
Exceeds eight (8) millions in the city.

The Holiday Blue's

Crowded streets, lightened shops, O what a festive atmosphere
Sweet laughter's ringing, from every corner.
Arm in arm the lovers stroll,
Looking deep into each other's eye
And I let out a mournful sigh, pondering why o why?
Joyous faces, happy children in well decorated stores
Must I walk around feeling sorry, feeling sore?
Help me, save me, if you can
For I got the holiday blue's.
The winter air, the falling snow, the fragrant perfumes
Alas! To loneliness, seems my fate is doomed.

Bits & Pieces of Conversation

In an Uptown Train
In a soft excited voice they carry on their conversations
As if your ears tuned to various radio stations
Asian, European, African and Latin
Wasp Muslims Gentile's and Jew
Omitting I am only a few.
Angry, agitated full of grudge
And you hear them all at once, what's the buzz?
The Chinese ladies speak their own dialect in a rapid tone
Two elderly men, by the door, their grievances out pour
Stone faced sits the Kansas native
Avoiding eye contact with the African man.
While at a distance not too far
Four young friends they laugh and joke
Indifferent of the crowd, Indifferent of their colors
Alas if we could only heed, to the message behind their laughter's.
And these diverse groups of people
Thrown together by greed's forceful hand
For a better understanding, a dialogue demands.
And they all get off on their respective stops
Unfinished phrases left behind, for someone else to carry on
And this human circus goes on and on ...... a never ending story
Uncomfortable truth and a human tragedy.

In search of the Artist

In this land of plenty
My pockets they are empty
In this land of the talented
Somehow I am un- wanted
I don't want to hear anymore or read about another millionaire
Rather bring me the news of that Artist dedicated and sincere
Tell me about his tiny garret
His Visions, His Dreams
His sadness abundant
Tell me how he looks.
His eyes, his clothes and his books
Does he have a divine countenance?
Describe me his pitied look at this world of appearance
His face I thirst to see
His words I long to hear
To feel His sacred presence I want to be near
Wherefore art thou, O Poet O Visionary?
Won't you deliver me to light from this darkness dreary?

Who Will Fix It?
Who Will Mend?

The meandering river
O my burning fever,
As the eagle tries to reach for the sun
My days on earth are done.
And yet it feels like I have just begun.

A loveless World
My desires trampled

Deceived too often
My resolves they have softened.

No dances, No joys
No happiness, Nor feasts

And we pretend……. and we pretend…
Till pretentious it is;
Mother Earth suffering from incurable disease.

O Great Creator your, World is broken
Who will pick up these broken pieces
Who will fix it? Who will mend?

A Modern Poem

The city heat
Crowded platforms;
Humming of machines,
And the telephone rings
Leave a message after the beep......
Music from the cafe
The curling smoke
From a burning cigarette
Cobbled streets
Whispering of friends
Soft Laughter's
A woman in high heels
The speeding highway
Sirens wailing
The last heart beats of a dying patient
A barking dog
A car comes to a screeching halt
Jolted to awareness.
The dryer on its spinning cycle
Endless Repetitions
Over
And
Over
&
Over again.

A Torn page from My Childhood

The days of serene innocence
Of carefree indulgence
In one's lazy thoughts and pranks.
The days of endless afternoons
With the sun blazing high in the midday sky.
Of curious snooping around, in cloudy afternoons.
The days when ignorance in the knowledge of complex human life
Was a blessing in disguise.
Alas! Nothing stays forever
And childhood must move on to adulthood and so forth.
But will I ever get back those days of pure serene innocence?

Far Away from the Civilization

Far away from the Civilization
Far away from the quarrels of all the Nation
A place untouched by businessmen
Where Nature prosperously reigns,
I want to go
Far away from the Civilization
Far away from all that is insane
Where pleasure overrides the pain
I want to go
That's where I would like to be.
Not plagued by worries, modern or mechanical
Where social behaviors are not affected neither artificial
That's where I would like to be.
Can you tell me where, I may find such a place
Where men and women are full of grace
Beauty lights up all their face;
And they know not what is vanity
Envy jealously hatred or disgrace.
That's where I would like to be.
Far away from the Civilization
Far away from the quarrels of all the Nation.

The Tale of John Kalahas

Once upon a time, there was
A man called John Kalahas
A country Man was he at heart;
Though he lived in the city.
Few years back, when loathsome fire,
Swallowed his farm;
With tears in his eyes:
He bade adieu;
To his family and Mother land.
Came he to the city, for search of work;
All he could manage was hard factory work.

Happy was John to have a job
So, he could send money, to his wife
And son Jacob.
Day in and day out, he toiled ever harder
Cutting corners here and there
So, he could again be a farmer;
Living happily with his family ever after!
But cruel destiny had something else in her mind.

The harder he worked,
With all the nuts, bolts and huge metal plates.
Less and less, was he able to contemplate.
With the passage of time,
The sensitive soul of John Kalahas,
Worn out in time.

And there emerged a new Kalahas
Hardened and Mechanized.
Before, John had reason
And passion in his life;
Now he drinks and gambles,
To forget the miseries of life;
When women and wine is,
Not enough for his ruins:
Often in sheer desperation
He runs to his beloved heroin.
Before, John Kalahas used to be a simple man
But now in intricate complexities
Is his life abound.

Then one day, a letter arrived,
From his village far away;
The gist of it was,
That his dear wife and son have passed away.
Nobody knows truly, the cause of death:
Though many speculated, emotional neglect
And lack of health.

A stormy thunderous night it was;
Shocked beyond belief was John Kalahas.
He remembered his ever green, sunny days.
The days of endless blue
Skies, warm summer nights.
And to his surprise,
The flood gates of sweet memories
Opened up again!
Filled with emotions and moved to tears:
The heartache and pain, he could to bear any further.

Next morning found, John Kalahas dead.
Thus the sad saga of John Kalahas ends.

9-11

The opening of elevator doors
Rustling of hurried steps on the carpet
The magnetic click of the office doors
A slow walk to the cubicle
To begin another long, weary day.
The dryness in the mouth quenched by black coffee,
What a satisfying gulp!
A fond, smiling glance exchanged with the picture of his wife and children
on the desk,
The first official call of the day
Thank God it's a friend!
Pleasant conversations, thrown backward and forward - interrupted with
laughter.
Suddenly a thundering crash shakes the building
Paper and debris flying everywhere
Fire and smoke engulf the floor
People scrambling for the Exit door
Chaos, Panic, Pandemonium and Mayhem.
Packed stairways filled with anxious people
Trapped workers screaming for HELP!
Brave firefighters and policemen rush in to save them.
Intense, unbearable heat and suffocating smoke
People jumping through 90 story windows, without any hope.

And their worst nightmare unfolds in front of them at a snail's pace
The bastard terrorists have attacked their office space.
Note: A poem dedicated to all the victims of this horrific tragedy and
specially to
Mr. Barry Kirschbaum
and Mr. Andrew Bailey

On the 93rd Floor of World Trade Center (my boss and my friend).

A Poem Dedicated to Peace

Peace thou God's beloved Angel!
When on Earth will you forever reign?
Behind every newborn's smile
You put all hope of lasting peace;
And again all your hopes are dashed
As they grow up, only to run after cash.

When will this hypocrisy end?
Only then, can peace on Earth descend.
Peace and prosperity goes hand in hand
Never do they both in one place stand
Like bees roaming from flower to flower
Peace and prosperity roams, distributing harmony and power.

Searching for peace all over the world
But it dwells in our hearts, innermost shrine;
Clear the dust and let it shine.
We substitute wars to justify peace
But how may bloody wars ever peace restore
Enough, Enough bloodshed! Please no more.

A day will soon to mankind dawn
The day when all forms of hostility is gone
No bitterness, no fights
No nationality and religions too.
In unison, we all will sing from our heart
Peace, Peace, Peace is here to stay at last.

I know it's a dream
That may never come true
But we must dream on
What else is there to do.
O Lord, Let Peace be still
Let it not be a flickering flame in gusty wind.